My State DELAWARE

By Christina Earley

TABLE OF CONTENTS

A Crabtree Seedlings Book

Crabtree Publishing
crabtreebooks.com

School-to-Home Support for Caregivers and Teachers

This book helps children grow by letting them practice reading. Here are a few guiding questions to help the reader build his or her comprehension skills. Possible answers appear in red.

Before Reading:

- What do I know about Delaware?
    - *I know that Delaware is a state.*
    - *I know that Delaware is a historic place.*

- What do I want to learn about Delaware?
    - *I want to learn which famous people were born in Delaware.*
    - *I want to learn what the state flag looks like.*

During Reading:

- What have I learned so far?
    - *I have learned that Dover is the state capital of Delaware.*
    - *I have learned that Rehoboth Beach was founded in 1873.*

- I wonder why...
    - *I wonder why the state flower is the peach blossom.*
    - *I wonder why they grow so many watermelons in Delaware.*

After Reading:

- What did I learn about Delaware?
    - *I have learned that Wilmington is the largest city in Delaware.*
    - *I have learned that the state animal is the grey fox.*

- Read the book again and look for the glossary words.
    - *I see the word **capital** on page 6, and the word **boardwalk** on page 15. The other glossary words are found on pages 22 and 23.*

DELAWARE

Hi! My name is Finn. Welcome to Delaware!

I live in Odessa. My town has a lot of very old buildings.

Odessa was built in the 1700s!

Delaware is in the eastern United States. The **capital** is Dover.

Fun Fact: Wilmington is the largest city in Delaware.

The state animal is the grey fox.

The peach
blossom is the
state flower.

We grow a lot of watermelons. They taste very sweet.

Fun Fact: Delaware **produces** 100 million pounds (45 million kg) of watermelon a year.

My state flag is blue. A gold diamond is in the middle.

The Delaware Blue Hens football team has won six national titles.

I like to visit Rehoboth Beach. I go for walks on the **boardwalk**.

Fun Fact: Rehoboth Beach was **founded** in 1873.

I can watch the sunset at Cape Henlopen.

I have fun seeing the animals at the Brandywine Zoo.

Astronomer Annie Jump Cannon was born in Delaware. WNBA **forward** Elena Delle Donne was also born in Delaware.

Fun Fact: President Joe Biden moved to Delaware when he was 10. He thinks of Delaware as his home.

I like to visit Fort Delaware. A tour of the fort lets me see what life was like there in 1864.

My family and I have fun exploring Fenwick Island.

Glossary

astronomer (as-tron-uh-mer): A person who studies planets, stars, and other objects in outer space

boardwalk (bord-walk): A wooden path built along a beach

capital (cap-ih-tuhl): The city or town where the government of a country, state, or province is located

forward (fawr-werd): A position on a basketball team

founded (found-ed): Created or set up

produces (pruh-doos-es): Makes or grows something for sale or use

Index

About the Author

Christina Earley lives in sunny South Florida with her husband and son. She enjoys traveling around the United States and learning about different historical places. Her hobbies include hiking, yoga, and baking.

Written by: Christina Earley
Designed and Illustrated by: Bobbie Houser
Series Development: James Earley
Proofreader: Melissa Boyce
Educational Consultant: Marie Lemke M.Ed.

Photographs:
Alamy: ZUMA: p. 13; ART Collection: p. 15, 23; Justin Cooper: p. 18 right, 23; IanDagnall Computing: p. 19
LOC: p. 18 left, 22
Shutterstock: BoothNCo: cover; bsankow: p. 3; Khairil Azhar Junos: p. 4; CM Glenn: p. 5; Volina: p. 6, 22; Real Window Creative: p. 7; moosehenderson: p. 8; canghai76: p. 9; kongsky: p. 10-11; 5 second Studio: p. 11, 23; railway fx: p. 12; Jon Bilous: p. 14-15, 22; kathleen collins: p. 16; Juhku: p. 17; Kelleher Photography: p. 20; George Sheldon: p. 21

Crabtree Publishing

crabtreebooks.com 800-387-7650

Printed in the U.S.A./012023/CG20220815

Published in Canada
Crabtree Publishing
616 Welland Avenue
St. Catharines, Ontario
L2M 5V6

Published in the United States
Crabtree Publishing
347 Fifth Avenue
Suite 1402-145
New York, New York, 10016

Library and Archives Canada Cataloguing in Publication
Available at Library and Archives Canada

Library of Congress Cataloging-in-Publication Data
Available at the Library of Congress

Hardcover: 978-1-0398-0244-5
Paperback: 978-1-0398-0254-4
Ebook (pdf): 978-1-0398-0274-2
Epub: 978-1-0398-0264-3